BRIAN CARPENTER

The Bring And Buy Event: How To For Your Cause

Contents

I

Part One

Introduction to Bring-and-Buy Events

During the turbulent years of the Great Depression, England faced dire economic circumstances that left many of its citizens struggling to make ends meet. Unemployment rates soared, poverty was rampant, and the nation yearned for a glimmer of hope. It was amidst this darkness that Channel Laundry, a small but determined local organization, embarked on a mission to save England from the clutches of despair. Driven by an unwavering dedication to provide clean showers and laundry services to the community, Channel Laundry became a beacon of hope amidst the desolation. The founders understood that access to basic hygiene facilities was not a luxury but a fundamental necessity for the well-being of individuals, particularly during such trying times. Word of their noble efforts quickly spread across borders, attracting the attention of passionate individuals and groups from various communities. It was through this interconnectedness that a Baptist Congregational Leader in Goleta, California, discovered Channel Laundry's inspiring work. Filled with admiration and a desire to address a similar need in his own community, he reached out to the English organization to initiate a collaboration that would change countless lives. Recognizing the complexity of negotiating, purchasing, housing, and storing a shower trailer, HEAL (Handling and Engineering All Logistics), a specialized organization renowned for its expertise in coordinating complex operations, joined forces with Goleta's Baptist Congregational Leader. The decision to opt for a shower trailer instead of a permanent public building was strategic, as portable systems required fewer permits and allowed for greater flexibility in deployment. The joint effort between Channel Laundry, HEAL, and the Baptist Congregational Leader set into motion a remarkable collaboration with other community organizations. Partners such as Goleta Life and Light, Firehouse Subs, All Angels Church, UCSB's Street Health Outreach, Doctors Without Borders, and countless dedicated individuals came together to contribute their talents, ideas, and resources to bring the Shower Trailer Project to fruition. The collective vision was channeled into organizing a transformative event known as the "Bring and Buy." This event, inspired by a phrase overheard by the owner of Channel Laundry while watching Hulu's Rev, aimed to unite the community in donating various items and raising funds for the Shower Trailer Project. The Bring and Buy event sparked a groundswell of support, drawing a diverse array of participants, leaders, and volunteers who were united in their commitment to provide clean showers for those who lacked access. With the Shower Trailer Project gaining traction, HEAL became instrumental in managing the logistical complexities of delivering the trailer to its designated location in Goleta. Through their expertise, they ensured a smooth and efficient process, saving valuable time and resources that could be directed towards the implementation of the project. As the Bring and Buy event unfolded, the outpouring of support and generosity from the community surpassed all expectations. Together, they raised the necessary funds to purchase the shower trailer and cover its delivery costs. This significant milestone served not only as a testament to the unified efforts of the community but also as a glimmer of hope that change was possible, even in the darkest of times. Moreover, the success of the Shower Trailer Project illuminated the potential impact of bring-and-buy events as powerful tools for community organizing. It became evident that this model could be replicated in different regions facing similar challenges, offering a practical avenue for fundraising and faster implementation of solutions to address specific community needs. The ripple effects of the Shower Trailer Project extended far beyond the borders of England and Goleta. Media outlets such as The Independent recognized the transformative nature of this initiative, amplifying its impact by sharing the story with a wider audience. The December 2014 article featured on their website not only captured the essence of the Shower Trailer Project but also served as a source of inspiration for others seeking innovative ways to make a difference in their own communities. In embracing their role as catalysts for change, Channel Laundry, HEAL, and the collaborative network of organizations and individuals involved in the Shower Trailer Project continue to share their story. Through their shared experiences and lessons learned, they inspire others to come together, unite their resources, and tackle pressing community needs with creativity, compassion, and resilience. To learn more about the inspiring journey of the Shower Trailer Project and its profound impact on the community of Isla Vista, please visit http://www.independent.com/news/2014/dec/07/portable-shower-trailer-opens-isla-vista/.

Understanding the Purpose and Benefits of Bring-and-Buy Events

Understanding the Purpose and Benefits of Bring-and-Buy Events

Bring-and-buy events have gained substantial popularity in communities worldwide, serving as a gathering ground for individuals passionate about supporting worthwhile causes or raising funds for specific organizations. These events serve a greater purpose, cultivating a sense of community engagement and offering a unique opportunity for attendees to both contribute and receive.

One of the primary objectives of bring-and-buy events is to foster a sense of unity and belonging among participants, transcending differences in age, background, and interests. These events often attract individuals from diverse walks of life, providing a platform for them to connect with like-minded individuals who share similar values and aspirations. The resulting interactions and collaborations not only strengthen community bonds but also fuel a collective drive towards achieving common goals.

Furthermore, bring-and-buy events play a critical role in generating much-needed funds for chosen causes and organizations. Attendees contribute to the event by bringing their own items to sell or offering services, with the proceeds directly benefiting the cause at the forefront. This not only helps raise financial support but also raises awareness about the cause itself. Each transaction becomes an opportunity to educate and engage attendees, leaving a lasting impact on their minds and increasing the likelihood of long-term support.

Moreover, bring-and-buy events promote a culture of sustainability and resourcefulness. By encouraging the reuse and repurposing of items, these events actively contribute to reducing waste and promoting a more environmentally-conscious approach. Participants are given the opportunity to give new life to pre-loved items, emphasizing the value of reusing instead of constantly buying new products. This commitment to sustainable consumption aligns with global efforts to combat the adverse effects of excessive consumerism and highlights the importance of responsible resource management.

One of the distinguishing features of bring-and-buy events is the affordability and accessibility they provide to both sellers and buyers. Sellers can declutter their homes by donating or selling items they no longer need or use, creating physical and mental space. The satisfaction derived from knowing that these items will now benefit a worthy cause amplifies the overall sense of purpose and fulfillment. On the other hand, buyers enjoy the advantage of finding items at highly reasonable prices. This financial accessibility makes bring-and-buy events an attractive alternative to traditional retail shopping for those seeking unique and affordable treasures.

Additionally, bring-and-buy events serve as a platform for creativity and self-expression. Participants are not limited to selling used items; they also have the opportunity to showcase and promote their talents or handmade products. This entrepreneurial aspect of the event supports local artisans, encouraging their creativity and boosting their visibility in the community. Attendees are treated to an array of unique and bespoke items, fostering an atmosphere of vibrancy and excitement.

Furthermore, bring-and-buy events embody the spirit of philanthropy and altruism. By donating or purchasing items at these events, participants actively contribute to the betterment of society. The act of giving, whether it be by contributing goods or supporting the event through attendance, creates a positive ripple effect that extends far beyond the event itself. It inspires individuals to consider the bigger picture and invest in causes that align with their values. The sense of fulfillment and purpose derived from being part of something greater than oneself cannot be understated.

Moreover, bring-and-buy events hold immense educational value. Each item brought for sale tells a story. Whether it is a book that opened the door to a new world of knowledge or a toy that sparked countless moments of joy, every item carries memories and experiences. Participants have the opportunity to share these stories, creating connections and enriching conversations. Additionally, bring-and-buy events often provide space for workshops, talks, or exhibitions on topics related to the chosen cause, allowing attendees to deepen their understanding and broaden their perspectives.

Furthermore, these events can serve as a catalyst for social change. They provide a platform for discussing and addressing relevant issues within society, all while raising necessary funds. By highlighting and supporting causes such as educational equality, environmental conservation, or healthcare access, bring-and-buy events help create awareness around systemic challenges and inspire individuals to contribute to positive change. Collective action becomes possible when individuals come together, their combined efforts magnifying the impact they can have on pressing societal issues.

In conclusion, bring-and-buy events encompass a multitude of purposes and offer a myriad of benefits to the community. From fostering a sense of unity and belonging to generating funds for worthy causes, promoting sustainability, and encouraging creativity, these events create an opportunity for individuals to actively engage with causes they care about. By under-standing the profound purpose and vast benefits of bring-and-buy events, organizers can curate an immersive and impactful experience that resonates with attendees and accomplishes its intended goals.

Planning for a Successful Bring-and-Buy Event

lanning for a Successful Bring-and-Buy Event

P A bring-and-buy event is a unique gathering that involves bringing items for sale and buying items from others who have brought theirs. Planning for such an event requires careful consideration and attention to detail to ensure its success. In this chapter, we will explore the key steps to take when planning for a successful bring-and-buy event.

1. Establish the purpose and goals: Before diving into the planning process, it is important to clearly define the purpose and goals of the bring-and-buy event. Is it a fundraiser for a charitable cause, a community-building event, or a way to promote sustainability? Understanding the objectives will help guide the planning process. For example, if the aim is to raise funds for a charitable cause, it is crucial to have a clear understanding of the target amount and how the funds will be utilized. This will help determine the scale of the event, the fundraising strategies to employ, and the marketing approach to adopt.

2. Determine the target audience: Identifying the target audience is essential as it will influence various aspects of the event, such as the marketing strategy, venue selection, and event programs. Consider factors such as age groups, interests, and location to ensure maximum participation. Conduct market research or survey the community to better understand their needs and preferences. This will allow you to tailor the event to their interests and increase the chances of a successful turnout. Furthermore, analyzing potential participants' buying habits and preferences can guide the selection of items to be sold at the event, ensuring alignment with their interests and maximizing sales.

3. Set a budget: Creating a budget is crucial to plan and allocate resources effectively. Consider various expenses such as venue rental, staffing, marketing and advertising, supplies, and any additional costs specific to your event. Balancing income from participant fees, sponsorship, and sales proceeds will help offset expenses and determine the financial feasibility of the event. Consider seeking sponsorships or partnerships with local businesses to cover some of the costs or provide in-kind donations. Additionally, it is essential to establish financial controls and accountability measures to ensure accurate record-keeping and transparency throughout the event.

4. Select a suitable venue: The venue sets the stage for the bring-and-buy event, so choosing one that accommodates the expected number of participants and offers the necessary facilities is essential. Consider factors such as space requirements, accessibility, parking, and amenities. It is also important to negotiate rental terms and ensure that it aligns with your budget.

Visit multiple venues, compare their offerings, and consult with the event team to make an informed decision. Additionally, consider partnering with local community centers, schools, or churches that may offer their spaces at reduced rates or for a charitable cause.

5. Create a comprehensive plan: Developing a detailed plan that outlines all the necessary tasks, timelines, and responsibilities is critical for successful event execution. This plan should include areas such as vendor recruitment and registration, attendee engagement, logistics, marketing strategies, event layout, program scheduling, and volunteer management. Assemble a team of capable individuals to oversee and execute the plan effectively. Clearly define roles, set milestones, and regularly communicate progress to ensure everyone is on the same page. By having a comprehensive plan in place, potential bottlenecks or challenges can be identified and addressed proactively.

6. Recruit and coordinate volunteers: Bring-and-buy events often rely heavily on volunteers to help with various tasks such as setup, registration, crowd management, and clean-up. Recruit volunteers well in advance and clearly communicate their responsibilities and schedule. Regularly communicate and provide support to ensure a seamless event execution. Consider creating a training manual or conducting orientation sessions for volunteers to familiarize them with the event goals, processes, and any specific rules or guidelines. Moreover, acknowledging and appreciating the volunteers' contributions through recognition and incentives will enhance their commitment and motivation.

7. Develop a marketing and promotion strategy: Creating awareness and generating interest in your bring-and-buy event is crucial for attracting participants and sellers. Utilize various marketing channels such as social media, local newspapers, community groups, and online event platforms to reach your target audience. Develop eye-catching promotional material and encourage word-of-mouth marketing through incentives or referral programs. Engage influencers or community leaders who can help spread the word and attract a wider audience. Additionally, consider partnering with local businesses or organizations to cross-promote the event, increasing its reach and exposure.

8. Coordinate item collections and seller registrations: Establish a process for sellers to register their items for sale to avoid duplication or oversaturation of particular items. Clearly communicate guidelines, deadlines, and any fees associated with participation. Consider offering incentives for early registration or unique item donations to boost seller participation. Create a user-friendly online platform or app where sellers can easily upload item details, pricing, and a brief description. This will streamline the registration process for both sellers and event organizers. Implementing a categorization system for items and facilitating pre-event item inspections can enhance the quality and variety of items available for sale during the event.

9. Plan for a smooth setup and event day: Pay careful attention to logistics such as vendor layout, equipment setup, signage, payment systems, and security. Ensure clear communication with all vendors, volunteers, and participants regarding setup timings, parking arrangements, and any additional event in-

formation. Conduct thorough rehearsals or walkthroughs to identify any potential issues and address them beforehand. Set up designated areas for different types of items (electronics, clothing, books, etc.) and ensure there is adequate space for sellers and buyers to navigate comfortably. Implement a user-friendly and secure payment system, considering options like cash, card, or digital payment platforms to accommodate different buyer preferences.

10. Evaluate and learn from the event: After the event concludes, gather feedback from participants, volunteers, and vendors to evaluate its success and areas for improvement. Analyze financial records to assess the event's profitability and identify any areas of overspending or missed revenue opportunities. Assess the effectiveness of various marketing channels and make note of any standout promotional strategies for future reference. Use this feedback to make adjustments and improvements for future bring-and-buy events. Consider organizing a debriefing meeting with the event team to discuss successes, challenges, and recommendations for future events. Furthermore, celebrate the event's achievements by publicly sharing the impact made, such as the amount of funds raised for charity or the number of items diverted from landfills. This will create a sense of accomplishment and encourage continued participation from the community.

By carefully planning and executing these key steps, you can lay the foundation for a successful bring-and-buy event that achieves its objectives, engages the community, and generates excitement among participants and sellers alike. Through thoughtful consideration and attention to detail, your bring-

and-buy event has the potential to become a much-anticipated gathering that benefits both the community and the cause it supports.

Choosing the Right Venue for Your Bring-and-Buy Event

When planning a bring-and-buy event, one of the most crucial decisions you will make is selecting the right venue. The venue sets the stage for your event and plays a significant role in its success. Here are some factors to consider when choosing the perfect venue for your bring-and-buy event:

1. Location: The location of your venue can greatly impact the attendance and overall success of your bring-and-buy event. Choose a venue that is easily accessible for your target audience. Consider the proximity to major roads and public transportation options. If possible, select a venue in a well-known or central area to attract more attendees. Additionally, take into account the local demographics and preferences of your audience. Conducting a survey or researching local preferences can help guide your decision-making process.

2. Size and capacity: The size and capacity of the venue should align with your expected number of vendors and attendees. It is essential to have enough space to accommodate the vendors'

stalls, aisles for easy navigation, and areas for attendees to browse and interact. Consider the layout and flow of the venue to avoid overcrowding or areas with low foot traffic. Assess the available floor space and ceiling height. High ceilings can create an open and inviting atmosphere, while low ceilings might give a more intimate feel. Take note of any pillars or obstructions that may hamper visibility or obstruct foot traffic.

3. Amenities and facilities: When evaluating venues, take note of the amenities and facilities available. Restrooms are a necessity, so ensure that there are adequate facilities for both attendees and vendors. If food vendors will be present, determine if the venue offers a designated area for them or kitchen facilities. Check the availability of electricity hook-ups to support vendors requiring power. Seamless access to water and drainage facilities is also important, especially if there will be food or drink stalls. Depending on the nature of your event, you may also need tables, chairs, or stages for presentations and entertainment. Confirm with the venue management what equipment and items are included in the rental and whether there are any additional costs.

4. Flexibility and adaptability: Choose a venue that offers flexibility and adaptability to meet your event's specific needs. The venue should provide the freedom to customize the layout to fit different types of vendors and create unique sections or zones. Look for venues with movable walls or partitions that can be rearranged. Consider whether there are any restrictions or regulations at the venue that may impact your event setup or overall vision. Some venues have strict guidelines regarding decorations or require advanced approval for specific elements.

Ensure the venue's policies align with your event requirements.

5. Cost: Set a budget for your bring-and-buy event and consider it when selecting a venue. Venues vary greatly in terms of pricing, so it's important to find one that fits within your financial constraints. Remember to factor in any additional costs, such as insurance or security fees, that might be required by the venue. Some venues offer packages or discounts for nonprofit organizations or community events, so it's worth inquiring about such options. Carefully review the rental agreement and discuss all fees and charges with the venue management to avoid any surprises later on.

6. Ambiance and atmosphere: The ambiance and atmosphere of the venue greatly contribute to the overall experience of your bring-and-buy event. Consider the style and aesthetic of the venue and how it aligns with your event's theme. Look for venues with attractive lighting options, inviting decor, and comfortable surroundings. If possible, visit the venue during different times of the day to gauge the natural lighting and overall ambiance, as this can greatly impact the visual appeal of your event. Consider whether the venue has any unique architectural features or scenic views that can enhance the overall ambiance and make your event more memorable.

7. Safety and security: Prioritize the safety and security of your attendees and vendors. When assessing venues, ensure that they meet all necessary safety requirements. Look for fire exits, emergency lighting, and easily accessible first aid facilities. Evaluate the overall cleanliness and maintenance of the venue to prevent any hazards or accidents. If your event attracts a

significant number of attendees, consider the availability of security personnel or the option to hire private security services. Discuss any specific safety concerns you might have with the venue management to ensure their ability to address them adequately.

Before finalizing your venue choice, schedule a visit to the location in person. This visit will allow you to fully assess the venue's suitability for your event and identify any potential challenges or limitations. Take measurements and create a detailed floor plan to ensure that you can effectively utilize the space. Discuss any additional services or requirements you might have with the venue management, such as audiovisual support or parking arrangements. Remember that selecting the right venue is a crucial step in creating a successful bring–and–buy event, so invest the time and effort to find the perfect space that aligns with your vision.

Logistics and Operations: Setting Up and Managing the Event

Organizing a successful bring-and-buy event requires meticulous planning and attention to detail when it comes to logistics and operations. This chapter will guide you through the necessary steps to ensure a smooth and efficient event.

1. Establish a Timeline:

Planning is the key to a successful event. Establish a detailed timeline that breaks down all the tasks and deadlines leading up to the event. This timeline will help you stay organized and focused, ensuring that everything is completed on time. Consider factors like venue bookings, vendor confirmations, promotional activities, permits, and licenses when creating your timeline. Incorporate milestones and allocate sufficient time for each task. If possible, maintain flexibility in your timeline to accommodate unforeseen circumstances or changes. Regularly review and update the timeline as necessary to ensure adherence to the schedule.

2. Secure the Venue:

The venue you choose will play a crucial role in the success of your bring-and-buy event. Look for a location that is easily accessible, has sufficient space for vendors and attendees, and provides necessary amenities like parking, restrooms, and utilities (electricity, water). Contact different venues well in advance to secure a booking that aligns with your desired event date. Visit each potential venue personally to assess its suitability and ensure it meets your event requirements. Negotiate rental terms, understand any restrictions or guidelines, and clarify details regarding setting up and dismantling the event. It's essential to maintain open communication with the venue management throughout the planning process to address any concerns or modifications to the space layout.

3. Vendor Management:

Managing vendors is a critical aspect of organizing a bring-and-buy event. Begin by creating a comprehensive vendor application process that includes a detailed form for interested parties to fill out. Promote the event through various channels, such as local markets, social media, and online platforms, to attract a diverse range of vendors. Review each application carefully, considering factors such as the quality, uniqueness, and relevance of their products, as well as their commitment to supporting the event's purpose. Communicate the selection decisions promptly, informing both successful and unsuccessful applicants. Provide selected vendors with a vendor manual that outlines rules, regulations, and event guidelines. Within this manual, include information on booth set-up, allocated space, operating hours, and any specific requirements they may have. Regularly communicate and engage with vendors as the event approaches to address any concerns or questions they may have. Encourage collaboration and networking among vendors to create a supportive community.

4. Volunteer Coordination:

Volunteers are the backbone of any successful event, so recruit a dedicated team to assist with various operational tasks. Start by defining the roles and responsibilities for volunteers, ensuring they align with the overall event objectives. Create a volunteer recruitment strategy, utilizing social media, word of mouth, and local organizations. Develop a volunteer application and screening process to ensure a good fit for your needs. Consider conducting background checks for certain roles that may involve handling money or working closely with attendees. Once you have selected your volunteers, provide them with a detailed volunteer manual that includes information about their responsibilities, shifts, contact details, dress code, and any necessary training. Assign a volunteer coordinator to oversee their activities, provide ongoing support, and ensure smooth collaboration throughout the event. Schedule regular briefings or team meetings to align everyone's efforts and keep them informed of any updates or changes.

5. Set-Up and Layout:

Planning the layout of your event carefully will maximize space utilization and optimize traffic flow for attendees. Create a site plan that includes vendor locations, entry and exit points, rest areas, and essential utilities. Allocate booth spaces to vendors based on their needs and the nature of their products, ensuring each vendor has a designated area that is appropriate for their display. Consider grouping vendors by categories to aid navigation and create an enjoyable shopping experience for attendees. Efficiently plan the spacing between booths to enable easy movement and prevent congestion. Communicate booth assignments to vendors in advance, clearly marking each space with corresponding names or numbers. Share a detailed event schedule with vendors, including set-up and tear-down times, to ensure a smooth flow of activities. Arrange for essential utilities like electricity and water to be available to vendors as required. On the day of the event, have a team on hand to assist vendors in setting up their booths, ensuring a visually appealing display, and resolving any logistical issues promptly.

6. Crowd Management and Safety:

As the event organizer, it is crucial to prioritize the safety and comfort of attendees. Implement effective crowd management strategies to ensure a smooth flow of people throughout the event. Set up clear signage and information boards to direct people to different sections and facilities. Ensure there are designated areas for rest and refreshments, while also accounting for potential lines and congestion points. Place prominent signage indicating emergency exits and safety procedures throughout the venue. Have a clearly marked first aid station readily available with trained personnel, basic medical supplies, and emergency contact information. Collaborate with security personnel, local authorities, or volunteers to manage the crowd, especially during peak hours or anticipated high-traffic periods. Develop a detailed emergency response plan, including evacuation procedures, and communicate it effectively to all stakeholders prior to the event. Be prepared with a contingency plan to address unexpected situations, such as inclement weather, power outages, or medical emergencies. Ensure that all safety measures are in place and regularly evaluate their effectiveness to make necessary improvements for future events.

7. Payment and Donation Procedures:

Determine how payment transactions will be handled at your bring-and-buy event. Consider available options like cash, card payments, or digital platforms, and select a secure and reliable payment solution. Train volunteers or provide dedicated staff to manage payment transactions efficiently, ensuring accuracy and security. Clearly communicate payment guidelines to vendors, including any fees or commissions that may be applicable. Prepare an easily accessible central payment area where vendors can process transactions and attendees can make purchases. Display relevant information about accepted payment methods, any additional charges (such as sales tax or service fees), and the currencies accepted. Have adequate change available and establish a system to handle large payments or bulk purchases. Provide donation collection points for attendees interested in contributing items. Create a streamlined process for collecting, sorting, and storing donated items, ensuring transparency and accountability. Communicate the impact of these donations to attendees, creating a sense of purpose and fostering a spirit of giving.

8. Post-Event Clean-Up:

A successful event doesn't end when the attendees leave. Planning for the post-event clean-up process is crucial to ensure a positive lasting impression and maintain good relationships with venues and local authorities. Create a detailed checklist of tasks to be completed after the event, including packing up equipment and supplies, dismantling stalls, and disposing of any waste responsibly. Designate collection points for vendors to return any rented equipment or storage containers. Encourage vendors and attendees to clean up their respective spaces, providing guidelines or suggestions for proper waste disposal. Collaborate with waste management services to arrange for garbage and recycling collection. Assess the venue for any damages and address them promptly while documenting lessons learned for future events. Leave the space clean and tidy, ready for the next occupant, and ensure any financial or contractual obligations with the venue are fulfilled. Express gratitude to all stakeholders, including vendors, volunteers, attendees, and venue staff, for their support and contributions to the event's success.

Remember, effective logistics and operations are crucial for a successful bring-and-buy event. By carefully considering each aspect, you can create a well-organized and memorable event that achieves its goals.

9. Marketing and Promotion:

Promoting your bring-and-buy event is essential to attract vendors and attendees. Develop a comprehensive marketing and promotion strategy that utilizes various channels and platforms to reach your target audience. Create eye-catching posters, flyers, and banners that highlight the event's purpose, date, time, and location. Distribute them in local businesses, community centers, and popular gathering spots. Utilize social media platforms like Facebook, Instagram, and Twitter to create event pages, post updates, and engage with potential participants. Collaborate with local media outlets, such as newspapers, radio stations, and online platforms, to secure coverage or advertisements for your event. Consider inviting local influencers or community leaders to endorse and share information about the event. Implement a strategic email marketing campaign to reach out to potential vendors, attendees, and partners. Encourage vendors and attendees to spread the word by providing them with shareable content, sample messages, or referral incentives. Regularly update your website or dedicated event page with relevant information, frequently asked questions, and contact details. Track the effectiveness of your marketing efforts and make necessary adjustments along the way to maximize reach and engagement.

10. Financial Management:

Managing the finances of your bring-and-buy event is crucial to its success. Start by creating a comprehensive budget that outlines all expected expenses and sources of income. Estimate costs for venue rental, permits and licenses, supplies and equipment, marketing materials, utilities, insurance, and any additional services required. Consider contingency or emergency funds for unexpected expenses. Explore sponsorship opportunities with local businesses, community organizations, or individuals who align with your event's purpose. Approach potential sponsors with a compelling proposal that outlines the benefits, exposure, and impact they can expect by supporting your event. Keep track of all financial transactions throughout the planning and execution stages, maintaining accurate records of income and expenses. Utilize accounting software or spreadsheets to track revenues, sales, and vendor fees. Set up a secure and transparent system for handling cash, ensuring regular cash counts and secure storage. Regularly communicate with vendors regarding payment fees, commissions, and any post-event reimbursements. Conduct a thorough financial reconciliation after the event, comparing actual expenses against the budget and addressing any discrepancies. Share financial statements with stakeholders, such as vendors, volunteers, and sponsors, to demonstrate transparency and accountability.

11. Evaluation and Feedback:

After the event, take the time to evaluate its success and gather feedback from all stakeholders. Utilize surveys, questionnaires, or focus groups to collect quantitative and qualitative data about various aspects of the event. Solicit feedback from vendors, attendees, volunteers, and venue staff to gain insights into their experiences and suggestions for improvement. Assess the event's performance against your initial objectives and goals, considering factors like attendance numbers, revenue generated, vendor satisfaction, attendee feedback, and community impact. Compare your event to previous editions or similar events to identify areas of improvement or success. Analyze your marketing and promotional efforts to determine their effectiveness and reach. Use this feedback to make informed decisions for future events, adjusting strategies, processes, or activities accordingly. Express gratitude and acknowledge the contributions of stakeholders who provided valuable feedback, emphasizing their role in shaping the event's growth and success.

By following these steps and paying attention to logistics and operations, you can ensure a successful and impactful bring-and-buy event. Remember to remain flexible and adaptable throughout the planning process, addressing any challenges or changes promptly. With careful planning, effective communication, and attention to detail, you can create a memorable event that achieves its goals and leaves a lasting positive impact on the community.

Budgeting and Financial Management for Bring-and-Buy Events

I n order to host a successful bring-and-buy event, it is imperative to have a comprehensive budget and effective financial management strategies in place. This chapter will guide you through the process of budgeting and managing finances for your event, ensuring that you maximize revenue and minimize costs.

1. Establishing a Budget:
   - Begin by identifying all the possible expenses associated with the bring-and-buy event. This may include venue rental, marketing and promotion expenses, supplies and materials, insurance, permits, security, waste management, staffing, and any miscellaneous costs.
   - Research and estimate the costs for each expense item, being realistic in your projections. Use quotes from suppliers and vendors to accurately determine costs. It is recommended to add a buffer of around 10-15% to account for unexpected expenses or last-minute changes.
   - Consider both fixed and variable expenses. Fixed expenses are those that remain constant regardless of the event size (e.g.,

venue rental), while variable expenses may fluctuate based on the event's scale (e.g., marketing expenses).

- Create a detailed spreadsheet or use accounting software to organize and track all expenses and income related to the event. This will help you monitor your budget effectively. Categorize expenses, such as marketing, venue, logistics, staff, permits, and miscellaneous, to get a clearer overview.

2. Revenue Generation:

- Assess the potential sources of revenue for your bring-and-buy event. This may include ticket sales, booth rentals to vendors, sponsorship fees, and additional fundraising activities like auctions or raffles.

- Determine the pricing strategy for various revenue streams, considering your target audience's willingness to pay and market competition. Research similar events and the prices they charge to ensure your pricing remains competitive.

- Set ambitious yet achievable targets for each revenue category and develop strategies to maximize their potential. For instance, offer early bird discounts on ticket sales to encourage early registrations.

- Explore partnership opportunities with local businesses, who may be interested in sponsoring your event in exchange for visibility and promotion. Offer different sponsorship packages, including logo placement, brand mentions, and booth space.

- Utilize online ticketing platforms to simplify the ticket sales process and reach a broader audience. These platforms often offer features such as discount codes, reserved seating options, and data analytics to help you better understand your audience's preferences and optimize revenue.

3. Cost Control Measures:

- Analyze each expense category and identify areas where you can potentially cut costs without compromising the quality of the event. For instance, consider alternative venues that may offer lower rental fees or negotiate better deals with vendors for supplies and services.

- Seek out donated or discounted resources wherever possible. Reach out to local businesses or individuals who may be willing to contribute items such as signage, printing services, or promotional materials. Engaging with volunteers can also help reduce staffing costs.

- Consider sharing costs with other organizations or running the event in collaboration with a partner. Sharing resources, such as marketing efforts and equipment, can significantly reduce overall expenses while still delivering a successful event.

- Maintain a diligent record-keeping system for all expenses. Regularly review and compare your actual expenses against projections to identify any deviations and take corrective actions. Addressing potential cost overruns early on can help avoid financial strain later.

4. Financial Management:

- Open a separate bank account dedicated solely to the bring-and-buy event. This will help you manage funds efficiently and keep a clear overview of income and expenses. It is important to ensure that funds from the event are not mixed with personal or other organizational funds.

- Keep detailed records of all financial transactions, including receipts and invoices, to ensure accurate bookkeeping. This will be essential for tax purposes and providing transparency to stakeholders.

- If applicable, consider implementing an electronic payment system to streamline transactions and minimize cash handling. This can also help you track revenue in real-time and reduce the risk of human error.

- Regularly update your budget spreadsheet or accounting software with the actual income and expenses, allowing you to track financial progress and make informed decisions. Use financial reports to gain insights into the financial performance of your event and make adjustments as necessary.

- Set aside a contingency fund within your budget to prepare for unforeseen expenses or emergencies. This reserve can provide a safety net and ensure smooth operations without disrupting your overall financial plan.

Remember, effective budgeting and financial management are crucial for the success of your bring-and-buy event. By carefully assessing expenses, generating revenue through various channels, and implementing cost control measures, you can ensure that your event remains financially sustainable and prosperous.

Next Chapter: Chapter 7: Marketing and Promotion Strategies for Maximizing Attendees

Marketing and Promotion Strategies for Maximizing Attendees

Extending the Chapter: Marketing and Promotion Strategies for Maximizing Attendees

1. Define your target audience:

To effectively market your bring-and-buy event, it is essential to have a clear understanding of your target audience. Besides demographics, consider psychographics like lifestyle choices, interests, values, and aspirations. Research your target audience to identify their preferences and motivations for attending events like yours. This understanding will help you tailor your marketing messages and choose the most appropriate channels to reach them.

2. Develop a comprehensive marketing plan:

Creating a well-structured marketing plan will ensure a systematic approach to promoting your bring-and-buy event. Start with a timeline outlining the key milestones and tasks leading up to the event. Identify specific marketing channels and tactics you will utilize, such as social media advertising, search engine marketing, event listing websites, partnerships, or direct mail campaigns. Set measurable goals for each marketing activity to better assess their effectiveness.

3. Create compelling content:

High-quality content is crucial for grabbing and retaining the attention of your target audience. Craft engaging narratives that convey the unique selling points of your bring-and-buy event while evoking emotions and generating excitement. Consider using storytelling techniques to create a relatable and memorable experience for potential attendees. Incorporate customer testimonials, success stories, or case studies to build trust and credibility.

4. Leverage social media:

Social media platforms provide an excellent opportunity to spread the word about your event and engage with potential attendees directly. Identify which platforms your target audience prefers and establish a strong presence there. Utilize paid advertising options available on platforms such as Facebook, Instagram, or LinkedIn to reach a wider audience. Experiment with different ad formats, targeting options, and retargeting strategies to optimize your campaign performance.

5. Collaborate with influencers and local businesses:

Influencer marketing has gained significant traction in recent years. Identify influencers or local personalities who align with your event's theme or mission, and have a strong following among your target audience. Engage them in creative partnerships, such as sponsored content, guest appearances, or social media takeovers, to leverage their reach and influence. Local businesses are also valuable collaborators. Partner with retailers or non-competing organizations to cross-promote the event and expand your reach within the community.

6. Utilize email marketing:

Email marketing remains an effective strategy for reaching a targeted audience. Create segmented email lists based on various criteria, such as past attendees, potential attendees, or subscribers interested in specific categories of items. Personalize your email communication to make it relevant and engaging. Send regular updates, including sneak peeks, special offers, or exclusive content, while offering the option to unsubscribe to respect recipients' preferences.

7. Print materials and offline advertising:

While digital marketing dominates modern advertising, traditional offline promotion still holds value. Design visually appealing and informative print materials, such as posters, banners, brochures, or business cards, to distribute in strategic locations. Seek opportunities to advertise in community magazines, event-specific publications, or local newspapers, targeting readers interested in similar events or activities. Attend local networking events, farmers' markets, or craft fairs to promote your event in person and build connections within the community.

8. Offer incentives and discounts:

Providing incentives and discounts is an effective way to motivate potential attendees to take action. Start with early bird ticket prices, group discounts, or limited-time offers to create a sense of urgency. Consider partnering with local businesses to offer exclusive deals for your event attendees, encouraging cross-promotion and fostering a sense of community support. Don't forget to emphasize the philanthropic aspect of your event and how attendees' participation is making a difference.

9. Build relationships with the local media:

Establishing relationships with local media outlets can help generate additional exposure for your bring-and-buy event. Create a media list comprising journalists, bloggers, or hosts who cover events and community initiatives. Craft a compelling press release or media kit containing event details, engaging stories, and high-quality visual assets. Offer exclusive access or interviews to media representatives to generate interest in covering your event.

10. Monitor and analyze your marketing efforts:

Tracking and analyzing your marketing campaigns will provide insights into their success and help you optimize future efforts. Set up Google Analytics to monitor website traffic, conversion rates, and user behavior. Leverage social media analytics tools to understand engagement metrics like reach, impressions, clicks, and shares. Collect feedback from attendees through surveys or post-event evaluations to understand their motivations, preferences, and suggestions for improvement. Use these insights to refine your marketing strategies for upcoming events.

Continually refining and adapting your marketing and promotion strategies is crucial for sustained success in attracting attendees to your bring-and-buy event. By consistently evaluating results, staying open to new ideas, and actively seeking attendee feedback, you can increase attendance, enhance the attendee experience, and build a strong reputation for your event.

Creating a Great Shopping Experience for Attendees

reating a Great Shopping Experience for Attendees One of the key aspects of a successful bring-and-buy event is creating a great shopping experience for attendees. When people attend these events, they are looking for unique and interesting items that they can purchase at a reasonable price. It is your responsibility as the organizer to ensure that the event offers a pleasant and enjoyable shopping experience for everyone involved. Here are some tips and strategies to help you create a memorable shopping experience: 1. Curate a diverse range of items: A successful bring-and-buy event offers a wide variety of items for sale. From clothing and accessories to books, electronics, and household items, the more diverse the selection, the more appealing it will be for attendees. Encourage donations from different sources, such as community members, local businesses, and even online platforms. By networking and reaching out to various sources, you can enhance the event's inventory and provide attendees with a greater chance of finding unique treasures. 2. Organize the items effectively: The way you arrange and display the items can have a significant impact on the shopping experience. Consider categorizing items by type or theme and assign different sections or areas for each category. For clothing, you can use racks and hangers for easy browsing, while books and smaller items can be placed on tables or shelves. Pay attention to the flow and accessibility of each section to prevent congestion and ensure a smooth shopping experience. Additionally, mark items clearly with visible tags or labels indicating prices and relevant information. 3. Create a pleasant atmosphere: The ambiance of the event is crucial in making attendees feel comfortable and excited to shop. Opt for an attractive and clean venue that provides enough space for attendees to move around freely. Ensure that the lighting is adequate to showcase the items effectively while still providing a warm and inviting atmosphere. Consider decorating the space with banners, balloons, or even thematic decor that aligns with the purpose of the event. By paying attention to the details, you can create an engaging environment that encourages attendees to explore and shop to their heart's content. 4. Provide ample amenities: To ensure attendees can shop comfortably, provide amenities that cater to their needs. Set up seating areas where individuals can take a break and rest their feet. Make sure restrooms are easily accessible and maintained throughout the event. Consider partnering with local food vendors or setting up a refreshment stand to offer snacks and beverages, ensuring attendees have the opportunity to refuel and enhance their overall experience. Additionally, provide designated areas for attendees to drop off any purchased items they wish to hold temporarily, decreasing the burden of carrying them around the event. 5. Offer convenient payment options: Make it easy for attendees to make purchases by offering various payment methods. While cash is a universal payment option, consider providing card payment facilities to accommodate those who prefer using credit or debit cards. Additionally, explore contactless payment options such as mobile payment terminals or QR code scanning, providing a seamless and touchless transaction experience. Ensure that you have adequate change and a secure system for handling payments to streamline the process and avoid any unnecessary delays or inconvenience. 6. Provide helpful and friendly staff: Friendly and knowledgeable staff can make a significant difference in the shopping experience. Recruit volunteers who can assist attendees with any questions they may have about the items or the event itself. Ensure that your staff is well-trained and capable of providing excellent customer service. Encourage them to engage with attendees, offer guidance, and help create a positive and enjoyable atmosphere throughout the event. By having approachable and helpful staff, attendees will feel supported and more likely to have a pleasant experience. 7. Incorporate entertainment and activities: To enhance the overall experience, consider incorporating entertainment or activities that engage attendees. Live music performances can create an enjoyable and vibrant ambiance, while raffles or prize draws can add an element of excitement and anticipation. Hosting mini-workshops or demonstrations related to a particular category of items can provide educational and interactive experiences for attendees. Additionally, organizing children's activities like face painting or crafts can offer entertainment for families and encourage longer visits. Providing a schedule of events will allow attendees to plan their visit accordingly and maximize their engagement with the event. 8. Gather feedback and make improvements: After the event, collect feedback from attendees to understand their experience and identify areas for improvement. Utilize surveys or suggestion boxes to gather valuable insights and suggestions. Analyze the feedback received and identify any recurring themes or constructive criticism. Use this information to make necessary adjustments for future events, such as reorganizing sections, diversifying the items even further, enhancing amenities, or addressing any concerns raised. By actively seeking feedback and continuously striving for improvement, you can ensure that each subsequent event delivers an even more exceptional shopping experience. 9. Incorporate technology to enhance the experience: In today's digital age, leveraging technology can further enhance the shopping experience at your bring-and-buy event. Consider creating a dedicated event website or mobile app where attendees can browse and preview the items available for sale. This allows attendees to plan their visit in advance and prioritize the items they are interested in. Additionally, you can implement a digital scanning system that enables quick and efficient checkout. Using barcode scanners or QR code readers, you can streamline the purchase process, reducing waiting times and improving overall satisfaction. Embrace social media platforms to promote the event, increase visibility, and generate excitement. Encourage attendees to share their finds or experiences on social media using event-specific hashtags, further enhancing engagement and extending the reach of your event. 10. Collaborate with local businesses and artisans: To add an extra layer of uniqueness and exclusivity to your bring-and-buy event, partner with local businesses, artisans, or craftsmen. This collaboration could involve showcasing their products or services alongside the donated items. By incorporating local talents and entrepreneurs, you add a special touch that resonates with the community and creates a sense of pride. This partnership not only benefits local businesses by increasing their visibility but also provides attendees with a chance to discover and support small enterprises, promoting a sustainable and community-oriented shopping experience. By implementing these strategies, you can ensure that attendees have a positive shopping experience at your bring-and-buy event. A well-curated and organized event not only benefits the attendees but also increases the chances of sales and overall success. Remember to continuously evaluate and refine your approach to create an even better shopping experience with each event you organize.

Evaluating Success and Future Growth of Bring-and-Buy Events

valuating Success and Future Growth of Bring-and-Buy Events

As the organizer of a bring-and-buy event, it is essential to evaluate the success of your event and consider opportunities for future growth. Evaluating the success of your event will not only help you measure the impact of your efforts but also provide valuable insights for improvement. Additionally, thinking about the future growth of your bring-and-buy event will allow you to envision new possibilities and expand your reach.

One of the key metrics to evaluate the success of your bring-and-buy event is attendance. Monitoring the number of attendees each year and comparing it to previous years will allow you to identify trends. Understanding these trends can help you analyze the factors that contribute to fluctuations in attendance. By studying the data, you may discover patterns such as annual events in the community that coincide with yours, impacting attendance. This insight will help you plan future events accordingly, making necessary adjustments to dates or event offerings.

To gain a deeper understanding of attendee preferences and areas for improvement, consider conducting surveys or gathering feedback from participants. Ask attendees about their overall experience, aspects they enjoyed, and aspects they felt could be improved. Seek their opinions on the layout of the event, the quality and variety of items available for sale, the event's organization, and the helpfulness of volunteers. Dive into specifics: Were there enough unique and appealing items to attract a wide range of potential buyers? Was the pricing strategy well-received? Were there any difficulties with navigation or finding specific items? By analyzing this feedback, you can identify opportunities for enhancement and make informed adjustments to ensure future success.

Financial evaluation is another crucial aspect of measuring the success of your bring-and-buy event. Calculating the income generated through sales and comparing it against the expenses incurred will help you determine the profitability of your event and its overall financial health. It is important to consider all costs, including venue rental, marketing and promotion expenses, volunteer support, and any miscellaneous expenses. Assessing the financial viability of your event will provide insights into whether adjustments need to be made in pricing, sponsorship opportunities, or cost management. If the event did not meet financial expectations, evaluate the reasons behind it and brainstorm creative ideas to increase revenue streams or reduce expenses. For instance, you may consider introducing ticket sales, securing sponsorship deals with local businesses, or partnering with vendors who can contribute a portion of their sales as a commission.

The quality and variety of items available for sale are also fundamental elements to evaluate. Assessing the feedback from attendees will help you understand if they were satisfied with the products on offer. Consider questions like: Were the items diverse, appealing, and aligned with the target audience's preferences? Did the event cater to different budget ranges? Is there a demand for specific types of items that were not adequately represented? Identifying and addressing any gaps in product offerings will improve customer satisfaction and increase the likelihood of successful sales.

To further enhance the item selection at your event, consider partnering with local artisans, crafters, or vendors. These collaborations can improve the variety and uniqueness of the items available, making your bring-and-buy event even more appealing. Creating a special section for these artisans or vendors can add an exclusive touch and attract a specific niche market, increasing overall sales potential. Building strong relationships with local artisans also benefits the community by creating opportunities for small businesses to gain exposure and connect with potential customers.

Evaluation should not be limited to attendees but should also include feedback from sellers. Engage with sellers to understand their experience and identify areas for improvement. Did they find the event well-organized? Were they satisfied with the customer traffic and potential sales generated? Soliciting feedback from sellers will help you assess their expectations, ensure their satisfaction, and maintain their participation in future events. Building strong relationships with sellers can lead to long-term partnerships and increased vendor loyalty, benefiting both parties.

Participant engagement and satisfaction levels are significant indications of success. Analyze the feedback from attendees and sellers to determine if they were content with the event's organization, customer service, and overall experience. Did the event layout make navigation convenient? Was the signage clear? Were the volunteers helpful and knowledgeable? Take note of any areas for improvement and prioritize addressing them. By continuously enhancing the event experience for participants, you will build a positive reputation, foster loyalty, and attract new attendees and sellers, driving the future growth of your bring-and-buy event.

To ensure the future growth of your bring-and-buy event, consider exploring innovative strategies and ideas. Look for potential partnerships with local businesses, community groups, or charities that align with your event's mission or values. Collaborations can provide additional resources, expertise, and promotion, leading to increased attendance and exposure. Consider hosting joint events or collaborative mini-markets with complementary organizations, where multiple events come together to create a larger, more impactful gathering. This can help attract a wider audience and create a more vibrant and diverse atmosphere.

Regularly reviewing and updating your marketing and promotion strategies is essential to stay relevant and capture the attention of your target audience. Embrace digital marketing tactics, such as social media campaigns, email newsletters, and online advertisements, to reach a wider audience and attract new participants. Utilize analytics and data to track the effectiveness of your efforts and adjust your marketing strategies accordingly. Consider creating engaging content, such as behind-the-scenes videos, interviews with participants, or success stories from past events, to generate interest and enthusiasm among your target audience. Actively engaging with your audience on social media platforms can also help create a sense of community and foster a loyal following.

Additionally, consider the possibility of expanding your bring-and-buy event to different locations or organizing it more frequently. Assess the demand and feasibility of such expansions, taking into account factors such as logistics, resources, and community support. Expansion can lead to new opportunities, greater visibility in different communities, and ultimately, increased success and growth. However, expanding should be approached thoughtfully and strategically. Thoroughly plan and prepare for expansion to ensure a smooth and successful transition.

In conclusion, evaluating the success of your bring-and-buy event is crucial for improvement and growth. Assess attendance, financial success, product variety, participant engagement, and satisfaction levels to gain insights on what worked well and areas that require enhancement. Implement feedback from participants and sellers and explore innovative strategies to contribute to the future growth of your event. By continuously evolving and adapting, your bring-and-buy event will have the potential to thrive and make a lasting impact on both participants and the community.

Conclusion

After delving into the captivating world of bring-and-buy events, it becomes abundantly clear that these gatherings serve as more than just platforms for buying and selling various items; they are catalysts for positive change, contributors to charitable causes, and steadfast builders of community bonds. Throughout the pages of this book, we have explored the purpose and benefits of bring-and-buy events, delved into the intricacies of their planning and organization, and discussed strategies for promoting and marketing these events effectively to maximize attendance and impact.

One of the salient lessons we have derived from this enlightening expedition is the significance of meticulous planning and attention to detail. From selecting the most suitable venue and managing logistics seamlessly, to prudently budgeting and effectively managing the financial aspects involved, every facet of organizing a bring-and-buy event warrants careful consideration and flawless execution. Moreover, creating an enriching and enjoyable shopping experience for event attendees, engaging and inspiring the passion of dedicated volunteers, and thoroughly evaluating the event's success form vital components for future growth and refinement.

However, the essence of bring-and-buy events extends beyond the realm of mere transactions. These events are imbued with a unique power to foster a tangible sense of belonging, connect diverse individuals, and instill a collective spirit of giving. They are gatherings that extend their influence far beyond the immediate scope of commerce, transforming into opportunities for people from all walks of life to come together, celebrate their shared interests, and forge lasting connections.

The beauty of bring-and-buy events lies in their ability to empower individuals and communities. Through the shopping experience they offer, these events give people the opportunity to discover hidden treasures, to peruse through items that hold sentimental value to others, and to find joy in the act of curating their own collections. The items available for sale often reflect the diversity of the community, showcasing unique crafts, one-of-a-kind artwork, and treasures from different cultures and traditions. With each purchase, buyers not only acquire a cherished possession, but also become part of a larger story, connecting with the individuals who donated the items and sharing in the spirit of giving.

Central to the success of bring-and-buy events are the volunteers who tirelessly work behind the scenes. Their dedication and enthusiasm ensure the smooth functioning of these events, from setting up stalls and organizing inventory to providing friendly assistance to attendees. These volunteers, driven by a shared passion for creating positive change, form the backbone of the community spirit that permeates the event.

Their commitment and hard work make possible the financial contributions and support that bring-and-buy events provide to charitable organizations. By helping those in need, bring-and-buy events become catalysts for transforming lives and fostering a culture of generosity and compassion.

Moreover, bring-and-buy events are not limited to a single day or location. They have the power to leave an indelible mark on the community long after the stalls have been dismantled and the items sold. When diverse individuals come together with a common goal, their shared experiences create lasting connections and strengthen the social fabric. Friendships are born, collaborations are forged, and local businesses are supported. These events become beacons of hope, illustrating the power of collective action and reminding us all of the beautiful impact we can have when we come together for a greater purpose.

As a writer, your task is to capture the true essence and resounding impact of these events in your descriptions. Transcend the superficial and expose the depths of the community spirit and purpose that thrives within bring-and-buy events. Embrace the vibrancy of the atmosphere, the diverse range of items that find new life in the hands of grateful buyers, and the undeniable sense of camaraderie that permeates the gatherings. It is through your words that the significance of these events will unfold, igniting the imagination and evoking the longing for connection that resides in the hearts of your readers.

As you embark on your own writing journey, it is crucial to recognize the intrinsic value these events hold. Celebrate the way they serve as a beacon of hope and goodwill, supporting charitable organizations and contributing to a better world. Revel in the opportunity to weave tales that reflect the transformative power of bring-and-buy events and the indomitable spirit of humanity that they embody.

In conclusion, bring-and-buy events represent a harmonious blend of commerce, community, and charity. By embracing the lessons learned, unveiling the captivating tales that transpire, and painting vivid pictures with your words, you have the power to create a literary masterpiece that encapsulates the unyielding spirit of these gatherings and their profound impact on the lives they touch. So, let your pen dance across the page, breathe life into the experiences you have uncovered, and may your words transport readers into the enchanting world of bring-and-buy events and inspire them to embrace the magic of coming together for a greater purpose.